The Growth Mindset

The New Psychology of world's top achievers and successful people for achieving massive success

By Ana Smitt

TABLE OF CONTENTS

Introduction 13
CHAPTER 1 14
    What is Mindset? 15
    How Mindsets Are Formed 15
    Types Of Mindsets 17
    Abundance Mindset vs Scarcity Mindset 18
    Productive Mindset vs Defensive Mindset 19
    Fixed Mindset vs Growth Mindset 21
CHAPTER 2 24
    Why is Mindset Important? 24
    Importance Of Mindset In Life 25
    Mindsets Are More Than Beliefs 27
    Life Experiences Reinforce The Mindset 27
    The Emotion Factor 29
    What Does Science Say About Mindsets? 29
CHAPTER 3 33
    Fixed vs Growth Mindset 33
    Mindset In Practice 34
    Mindset In Action 35
    The Basics of Fixed vs Growth Mindset 37
CHAPTER 4 42
    The Dangers of a Fixed Mindset 43
    Undermining The Importance Of Effort 44
    The Obsession To Prove Worth 45
    The Desire To Be Flawless 46

- Decreasing Self-Knowledge 47
- The Need for Constant Validation 47
- The Power of a Growth Mindset 53
- Improvement Through Effort 54
- Offers A Sense Of Fulfilment 55
- Develops Resilience 55
- Buffers Against Demotivation 56
- Encourages Perseverance 57
- Promotes Critical Thinking 58
- Practice Makes Perfect 59

CHAPTER 6 63
- Can You Change Your Mindset? 63
- Resistant To Change 63
- Using Fear To Change Your Mindset 64
- Using Actions To Change Your Mindset 65
- Identifying Your Counter Mindsets 66
- Shifting Gears From The Negative To The Positive 68
- Understand "WHY" You Need To Change 68
- Start Small To Finish Big 71

CHAPTER 7 74
- Strategies to Develop a Growth Mindset 74
- Continual Learning 74
- Be Committed 75
- Develop Healthy Self Esteem 76
- Work On Your Perspective 77
- Set Effective Goals 78
- Manage Your Inner Negative Voice 79

Facing Adversity 80
Be Open To Feedback 80
Dealing with Setbacks 84
The Importance Of Failure 85
Experience And Knowledge 86
Resilience And Growth 86
Change Your Strategy 87
Seeking Inspiration Through Others 87
Using Failure As Leverage 88
Redefining Priorities And Values 89
Don't Let Your Failure Define You 89
Helps Reach Your Potential 90
Failure Is Always Better Than Regret 90
Setbacks Yield A Sense Of Direction 91

CONCLUSION 92
THANK YOU FOR READING MY BOOK! 93
ABOUT THE AUTHOR 95

THANK YOU FOR YOUR PURCHASED !

This Book (VALUE $17) Is Yours FREE!:

You'll Discover...

1. The Science Behind Successful Mindset - How To Be Insanely Successful and Confident

2. 5 Ways To Develop The Mindset of A Champion

3. Mindsets Hacks To Achieve Your Goals 10X Faster

>>> DOWN LOAD YOUR BONUS HERE ! <<<

The Growth Mindset

Copyright 2018 by Ana Smitt - All rights reserved.

ISBN: 9781717714374

This document is geared towards providing exact and reliable information in regards to the topic and issue covered. The publication is sold with the idea that the publisher is not required to render accounting, officially permitted, or otherwise, qualified services. If advice is necessary, legal or professional, a practiced individual in the profession should be ordered.

- From a Declaration of Principles which was accepted and approved equally by a Committee of the American Bar Association and a Committee of Publishers and Associations.

In no way is it legal to reproduce, duplicate, or transmit any part of this document in either electronic means or in printed format. Recording of this publication is strictly prohibited and any storage of this document is not allowed unless with written permission from the publisher. All rights reserved.

The information provided herein is stated to be truthful and consistent, in that any liability, in terms of inattention or otherwise, by any usage or abuse of any policies, processes, or directions contained within is the solitary and utter responsibility of the recipient reader. Under no circumstances will any legal responsibility or blame be held against the publisher for any reparation, damages, or monetary loss due to the information herein, either directly or indirectly.

Respective authors own all copyrights not held by the publisher.

The information herein is offered for informational purposes solely, and is universal as so. The presentation of the information is without contract or any type of guarantee assurance.

The trademarks that are used are without any consent, and the publication of the trademark is without permission or backing by the trademark owner. All trademarks and brands within this book are for clarifying purposes only and are the owned by the owners themselves, not affiliated with this document.

Introduction

In this world, you're either GROWING or you're DYING... There's no middle ground. If you're standing still with zero progress, you're decaying. The same goes for success. It requires you to engage in the process of your personal growth at all times. And of all the things in life, what you believe about yourself can impact your success or failure.

People who believe that their abilities can be improved through their hard work and dedication typically move ahead and take action without coming up with excuses. These same people also demonstrate an open mind, are willing to learn and have been seen as most successful in different aspects of their life. So how do they do it?

This book will tell you how. You will see that the mind is the ultimate force to get you where you want to go but you need to harness its power correctly. How can you do that? Let's find out together.

CHAPTER 1: WHAT IS MINDSET?

CHAPTER 1

What is Mindset?

The mind is a very powerful tool and it ultimately determines who you are as a person. Also known as mindset, this thinking pattern or your frame of mind impacts how you make sense of the world as well as of yourself.

So in other words, a mindset is a set of beliefs and thoughts which influence the way you handle any given situation. It pretty much dictates your personality helping you sort out what's going on around you and what you should do about it.

How Mindsets Are Formed

Since time immemorial, people have thought, acted and fared differently from one another. For the most part, common sense dictates that these differences arise from the variances in one's background, learning experiences and training. Plus, research also points in the same direction.

So while experiences, backgrounds and training are all external variables, even internal variables like genetic makeup have a part to play.

The Growth Mindset

Most experts today agree that forming a mindset is a combination of the two. For instance, while everyone comes with a unique set of genetics, their experiences, training and personal efforts take them the rest of the way.

So your life experiences and genetics together help frame your attitude and beliefs. And since both have an important part to play in your mindset, it helps to know what these two factors are all about.

First off, your attitude to something is how you think or feel about it, especially when it shows in the way you behave.

Your attitude can have different components such as an emotional component or how something or someone makes you feel. Then there is the cognitive component which is how or what you think about the subject. This is finally followed by the behavioral component which shows how you behave when confronted by the subject.

Then there are your beliefs which are merely feelings of certainty about something. Beliefs are based on ideas and when at a specific point, these ideas start to feel certain, they turn into beliefs. Beliefs, in turn shape your attitude which in turn shape your mindset.

Attitudes and beliefs then give rise to habits which are a direct reflection of your mindset.

Perhaps the most common and well known example of a mindset is seeing the glass as "half empty" or "half full".

Types Of Mindsets

There are different types of mindsets that can either help you unleash your best or contain your potential. There could be a long list of these but here are a few which have been backed by research. Here's a quick glance at the following:

The Growth Mindset

Abundance Mindset vs Scarcity Mindset

The way you view abundance or scarcity in different aspects of life greatly influences your success in life, For instance, imagine that two people are walking down the street. They are talking to each other, laughing, joking and all the while breathing in and breathing out.

Now do you think that one of the two might worry that there may not be enough oxygen for the both of them? Likely not, since air is abundant.

Now place the same two people scuba diving where one's tank starts to malfunction. That person signals the need for oxygen and suddenly the air around them becomes a precious commodity.

This scarcity could easily make the two worry with a concern that what if there isn't enough oxygen for the both of them?

For the most part, the general population seems to be more inclined towards a scarcity mentality. They often view life as having only so much and if they had to share, there wouldn't be enough for them.

This sad mentality makes it very hard for such people to share anything including credit, recognition, responsibility or even authority with others. Instead they only end up competing for available resources even when there may be an abundance of them.

On the other hand, those with an abundance mentality are not limited by this thinking pattern. Instead of seeing opportunity as limited, they strive to create more opportunity for themselves and embrace change instead of fearing it.

To sum up, a person with a scarcity mindset chooses negative thoughts and adopts a victim mentality. At best, their everyday focus is on all the things that may not be working.

But others with an abundance mindset tend to put all their energy reserves into what is working and see endless possibilities to improve their current situation.

Productive Mindset vs Defensive Mindset

This combo basically deals with everyday performance. Many people may think that they have a productive mindset or that they are being productive, whereas they are actually just being busy; in reality, they may not be productively finishing tasks and completing projects.

The Growth Mindset

Think about your daily to-do list and the ten or so things you need to get done by the end of the day. You may have spent all your day running around and 'doing' stuff but when it's 5 pm and you wrap up for the day, you realize that you only managed to tick off three of the ten things you were supposed to do. You feel like you're working all the time but don't actually get much done.

Does this mean that you're lazy and don't want to achieve your goals? Or perhaps it has something to do with your mindset.

Having a productive mindset means that you utilize all your resources including your time, energy and efforts in the best possible way. At the same time it also means that you don't try to do everything, be everywhere or even do it in the fastest way possible.

Quite the contrary, it means making the most of what is available while enjoying the process. Those with a productive mindset seek out valid knowledge that is testable and use their reasoning to make informed choices.

As such, these people find a way and spend more time finding solutions to better performance instead of finding problems and getting stuck.

On the other hand, the defensive mindset, like its name suggests is both self-protective and self-defensive. This type of mindset only seeks out information that it feels comfortable with and shuts down

when perceived as threatening. Obviously this thinking pattern can become very limiting.

It's also an apparent way to shun creativity, find better alternatives to existing problems and very easily fall in a rut. But perhaps the biggest setback of this mindset is that you learn something based on false assumptions or prevent learning altogether.

Fixed Mindset vs Growth Mindset

This combo is perhaps the best known in terms of mindsets. Very briefly, a fixed mindset is a static view where you believe that you are either good at something or you just aren't, with no way to change that so called 'Fact' or 'Destiny'.

On the other hand, a growth mindset is a learning mindset with a dynamic view. This mindset allows you to believe that you can change, improve, prosper and get better at anything through the right training.

The Growth Mindset

Now going back to the three pairs of mindsets, it's fairly easy to see that one mindset from each pair allows you to explore, grow and be more content in general. The other does the opposite.

These limiting mindsets may appear to offer more comfort, be easier to follow and require less effort but do come at a cost. Not only do they repel the good opportunities in life but can also hold you back from achieving your full potential.

CHAPTER 2

Why is Mindset Important?

Now every mindset can work in a dual manner. For instance, while your individual mindset can open doors for you, it can also set serious limitations based on your beliefs and approach in different scenarios.

This means that just as mindsets can help you spot opportunities, they can equally well trap you in self-defeating cycles as well. The stories that you tell yourself and the things that you believe about yourself can go either way.

First off, if you become trapped in a negative or limiting mindset then your mindset will prevent change from happening in your life. But if you develop a positive mindset then you allow new skills to blossom.

The Growth Mindset

Importance Of Mindset In Life

Because your mindset holds your set of beliefs, it has immense potential to make a difference in your life. For most people their beliefs are the core of their efforts. As such, beliefs distinguish people who are successful at what they do as opposed to others who continually struggle.

These beliefs form the basis of where your abilities come from. Just think about your talents, your intelligence, and your personality. Do you consider these traits to be simply fixed and permanent, or do you think these are aspects which you can cultivate and improve on through life?

The rigidity or flexibility about these beliefs is what determines your mindset.

Having the right mindset for any particular task is almost a prerequisite for success. Whether you're a parent, teacher, student, entrepreneur, or in any other profession, you need the right mindset to be successful at what you do.

Every profession comes with its own hurdles and obstacles and having a positive mindset allows you to not only overcome those obstacles but even welcome them as challenges or an opportunity to learn and grow.

If you look around you, you'll see that often people with similar circumstances have very different results in life. This happens because of their mindset.

Since your mindset regarding events and situations influences your interpretation of them, the results will be different from someone else with a different mindset.

If you've got a positive mindset, you'll find it easier to overcome setbacks than others with a negative or limiting mindset. Or, if you have a negative mindset, you'll feel the world collapse under your feet every time there is an unpleasant experience.

If your core beliefs don't support you, then you'll likely set yourself up for failure when faced with a difficult situation. You may be more susceptible to surrendering and admitting failure when all you need to do is try harder or perhaps take on a different approach. You may also need to change your frame of mind.

The Growth Mindset

Mindsets Are More Than Beliefs

But mindsets aren't mere beliefs and have the capacity to dictate your reactions to situations and other tendencies. They serve a number of cognitive functions and let you frame situations. At the same time, your mindset will also direct your attention to the most important cues and filter out irrelevant information so that you don't overwhelm yourself.

Your mindset will also give you direction by recommending sensible goals to achieve so that you have a sense of direction. Once your mindset becomes habitual, it defines who you are and what you can become.

Life Experiences Reinforce The Mindset

For the majority of people, their mindset is created for them at an early age. It may be through parents, teachers, friends or others that you readily absorb what you are told.

The Growth Mindset

And because when you're young and have no other point of reference, you accept the offered knowledge. This basic information then becomes embedded within your psyche and starts to shape your beliefs about the world and your place within it.

As you grow and mature, life experiences and events may contradict that earlier knowledge and somewhat change your mindset. However, the earlier knowledge continues to stick and becomes your reference point for much of your life. For instance, if you're surrounded by people who are in a constant state of anxiety and overwhelm then there's a good chance that you'll develop a mindset that mirrors reactions to life in ways that are anxious and overwhelmed.

Your mindset continues developing and becomes stronger the more you repeat and practice your beliefs.

Now if you become locked in a negative or limiting mindset, then you'll likely keep repeating negative self-talk and start to see things in a certain way. This practice can become self-fulfilling until you completely believe it to be true.

On the other end of the spectrum, if you have a positive mindset then it gets reinforced through your beliefs and consequent actions.

The Emotion Factor

However, repetition isn't the only factor at play in the creation of habits and beliefs. The emotion factor also plays in this equation. When you mix repeated thoughts and actions with emotions, the expected results can alter.

Both helpful and bad habits get created the same way- through repetition. But the habit can be embedded more quickly and strongly when combined with emotion.

Take the example of comfort eating. You know that it's not good for you but since it makes you feel good at a time when you are down, you turn to this habit to lift up your spirits. Once you get into this cycle, you develop a behavior paired with powerful emotion and an unhealthy eating habit is formed.

What Does Science Say About Mindsets?

Neuroscience or the study of the nervous system tells us that the brain is continually creating and destroying neural pathways. These pathways, in turn, form our thoughts and behavior patterns which tell your brain to make decisions, choose actions and present you to the outside world.

The Growth Mindset

Among these, the pathways which are used more become stronger, while others that remain underused become weak and ultimately get replaced.

This scientific data correlates with the explanation of different mindsets because the brain is prewired with the bias to learn new things. At the same time, there are also those people who learn to stop learning and become trapped in a fixed mindset.

People with positive mindsets are more likely to improve which reinforces the thought that ability can be enhanced. On the flip side, people with a negative mindset appear to stagnate which reinforces the thought that they get stuck at their current ability level with no improvement.

These two particular are of concern to us in this book and are known as the growth mindset and the fixed mindset. The difference between the two is that while one focuses on the results achieved, the other stresses on the process.

The fixed mindset prioritizes results such as getting "that job" or losing "those 30 pounds" where the person thinks that they are defined by the result. The growth mindset tells you that the effort put into the process of achieving that result is more important.

The Growth Mindset

This is because you can become more intelligent, more creative, and more successful by focusing on the process and not the outcome. It leaves a lot of room for improvement which means you continue to grow as a person.

Going forward, let's take a closer look at each type.

CHAPTER 3

Fixed vs Growth Mindset

By now you know that the way you think about your ability has a very real impact on the results you achieve in life. Interestingly enough, both fixed and growth mindsets are highly self-reinforcing, but in vastly different ways.

If you believe that ability is an ingrained or fixed feature which you were born with and can't change, then you possess a fixed mindset. But if you think that you can develop this ability through effort and practice then you have a growth mindset.

Each belief leads to different behaviors and consequently different results. Of the two, having a growth mindset, where you are ready and willing to learn and improve, is the key to success.

Having said that, it doesn't imply that hard work, persistence and struggle aren't important. They are, but only when you believe that you aren't limited and are in full control of your destiny.

The Growth Mindset

Mindset In Practice

Individuals with these two mindsets not only think differently but also react to information in a different manner. In fact, the differences can be stark when they respond to information about

performance.

For instance, people with a fixed mindset respond very well to information about how well they have done something. It could be anything from trying out a new recipe, learning a new language, working on a DIY project, or doing well on test results and grades.

The Growth Mindset

Their minds are most active when they learn about their good performance. Their prime, but somewhat limited concern is with the results achieved with stress on the praise they receive.

On the other hand, people with a growth mindset tend to be most responsive when they are told about the ways they could improve their performance. These folks want to learn how to better themselves which leaves a lot of room for growth.

They are more interested in strategies to help them evolve and the process of doing so, not merely their talent or ability.

The two are, in fact very different approaches, with the former being focused on "How did I do?" as opposed to the latter which deals with "What can I do better next time?"

The fixed mindset is all about how the performance was perceived and the growth mindset is about how improvement can take place. It isn't hard to see which mindset will yield better results in the long run.

The Growth Mindset

Mindset In Action

When it comes to taking action, both the fixed as well as the growth mindset are also poles apart. To refer to a very well-known example, let's take the story of the tortoise and the hare.

In the story, the hare was so certain that he could win that he sat down and went to sleep during the race. On the other hand, the tortoise was persistent and kept going believing that that he had a chance of winning.

When the hare woke up, he started running as fast as he could but he was just too late. In the meantime, the tortoise had won.

So the story shows that the hare had a fixed mindset where he believed that his inherent ability for speed would guarantee a win. But the tortoise showed a growth mindset where he believed he needed to work hard to get to a certain point. At the same time, he was not afraid of failure but ready to take on a challenge.

This also points out to the fact that a fixed mindset can be susceptible to an overly perfect finished view of oneself. Much like the hare, this thinking pattern suggests that you are already perfect.

And so your brain becomes less adept at recognizing opportunities for improvement.

The Basics of Fixed vs Growth Mindset

People with a fixed mindset accept their traits as a given. They believe there is a certain amount of intelligence and talent and there is nothing that can change this fact. So people with this mindset are often concerned about their traits and how adequate they are.

With a fixed mindset you believe that your ability is innate and you find failure unsettling as it makes you question how good you really are. Another belief shared by people with this mindset is that there's a hidden upper limit to what you can achieve.

For instance, if you've struggled through school, you may well believe that you're not cut out for college. You may never even try out for college but get stuck in a low paying, non-engaging job instead. Such a job won't do anything for stimulating your brain and the belief of inadequacy becomes your reality.

The Growth Mindset

On the other hand, if you have a growth mindset, then you accept that you can improve your ability and failure only tells what you should work on.

Those who have a fixed mindset are all about proving themselves and often become defensive should anyone point out that they made an error. This mindset only allows people to measure themselves by their failures.

The growth mindset, on the other hand often exhibits resilience and perseverance in the face of errors. Instead of adopting a defensive approach, they become motivated to better their performance.

Take a look at these state of mind statements by people with a fixed and growth mindset:

The Growth Mindset

Fixed mindset

I'm horrible at math.

I can't seem to get organized.

I love cake, but I can't bake.

I'm no good at origami.

Growth mindset

Math has been challenging for me.

I've tried my hand at organization, but without much success.

I'd like to learn baking, but I haven't started yet.

I haven't learnt how to do origami yet.

The Growth Mindset

It's easy to see from these examples that quotes from the fixed mindset group are more of a statement of resignation such as "horrible at", "can't seem to", "can't bake" and "no good at". There's an implied unwillingness to try as the person believes that these skills are beyond their scope. A sense of finality prevails within this group.

The growth mindset group presents examples which are more of an observation than a statement. These opinions reflect that there is the possibility of learning a skill if the person puts in some more effort and tries harder.

So when distinguishing the fixed mindset from the growth mindset, keep the following in mind:

Goals: The fixed mindset wants to look smart whereas the growth mindset wants to learn and improve.

Challenge seeking: The fixed mindset avoids challenges but the growth mindset seeks it out.

Change: Change is seen as a threat by the fixed mindset but the growth mindset views the same as a challenge.

The Growth Mindset

Response to setbacks: People trapped in a fixed mindset respond poorly to setbacks, appearing helpless but those with a growth mindset appear resilient.

Response to criticism: The fixed mindset will appear defensive when faced with criticism but the growth mindset will learn from it.

Response to wrongdoing: The fixed mindset tends to punish and retaliate in this situation whereas the growth mindset tends to educate and compromise.

Viewing others' success: The fixed mindset views others' success as a threat but the growth mindset sees it as inspiring.

The Growth Mindset

CHAPTER 4
THE DANGERS OF A FIXED MINDSET

CHAPTER 4

The Dangers of a Fixed Mindset

The advantages of a growth mindset may seem apparent, but many people have a fixed mindset in certain situations. This can be very counterproductive because this mindset prevents important skills from developing and growing. This, in turn sabotages your happiness and health in the future.

As an example, let's assume that you aren't a science whiz. If you keep telling yourself that you aren't a science person or that science isn't your thing, then that assertion becomes an excuse to not study science.

While with a fixed mindset, you may avoid short term failure, you are also hindering your potential to grow, learn and acquire new skills in the long run.

The Growth Mindset

On the other hand, your peer with a growth mindset tries to give science a go despite failing at first. Now this person likely sees failure as a sign to continue working on their skills instead of accepting that they aren't good at something.

In the long run, your peer will optimize their potential as they chose to benefit from criticism instead of ignoring it. They decided to overcome a challenge instead of avoiding it and see it as a learning opportunity rather than feeling threatened.

So if you think things like "It's impossible to lose the weight", "I'm not a natural artist", "I'm not creative", or "I'm a procrastinator" then you'll miss out on many experiences. In the end, you quit, don't learn as much and it becomes decidedly harder to get any better.

Here are other aspects you'll miss out on:

Undermining The Importance Of Effort

In a fixed mindset, basic qualities, such as talent or intelligence are considered fixed traits. Such individuals have a tendency to document their talent or intelligence rather than develop them. They may also credit talent alone to success, without effort. When they are good at something, they gladly attribute it to their talent such as scoring high on a test or doing well on a project.

However, at the same time, they also consider their shakier skills to be fixed as well. So instead of developing these skills they tend to accept them as is with no effort invested on improvement, such as "I'm not cut out to handle a paint brush".

They accept that they are the way they are and can't get any better at it or change.

The Obsession To Prove Worth

People with a fixed mindset feel a need to prove their worth. Every scenario demands a confirmation of their personality, intelligence, or character.

Every scenario is also overly evaluated resulting in questions like "Will I succeed or fail?", "Will I look dumb or smart?", "Will I be rejected or accepted?" and so on.

The Growth Mindset

Although they seem desperate for approval, they aren't going to go beyond their capabilities to achieve the success they want so badly. They tend to get stuck because they're terrified of being rejected that they're not willing to grow beyond their shell.

The Desire To Be Flawless

Taking it a step further, the problem with a fixed mindset is that it is not enough just to succeed neither is it enough to look smart and talented. If anything, the desire is to appear pretty much flawless.

So what happens in the end is that if failure means you lack potential or competence, then you are stuck being a failure. There is nowhere to go from this point.

Instead you end up focusing on avoiding failure at any cost and try to preserve feelings of success. You don't try anything new because if you don't think you'll excel at it, you don't want others to see you fail. In the end, the entire process can be very restricting and frustrating.

Decreasing Self-Knowledge

Perhaps one of the most damaging effects of a fixed mindset is that it decreases self-knowledge. Instead the focus shifts to external rewards and validations. With this mindset, attention is taken away from internal development.

By constantly striving for external recognition and signs of success, you tend to deceive not only others but yourself as well. It also takes away from who you really are.

The Need for Constant Validation

Your mindset can also impacts your relationship with others. Often individuals with a fixed mindset feel insecure and expect their partners, friends, peers and others to support them in every situation.

The Growth Mindset

They only want to be around people who praise them for their skills and give them confidence they were unable to establish for themselves. However, this can present problems for what if the romantic liaisons end, friendships fall out or conflict arises among peers?

Any of these situations would leave a person with a fixed mindset with low esteem, poor confidence and a lot of doubt and fear.

To summarize, here is how a fixed mindset looks at things:

The Growth Mindset

Skills: The fixed mindset believes this is something you're born with which can't be changed.

Challenges: The fixed mindset regards this as something to avoid at all costs. There is the constant threat that a challenge could expose your lack of skill and you tend to give up easily when in such position.

Effort: This is considered unnecessary by the fixed mind. It's something that people resort to when they aren't good enough for the job.

Feedback: Feedback makes the fixed mindset get on the defensive. When given feedback, people with this mindset take it personally and consider it an exclusive attack on their performance or skills. If it isn't to their liking they may even ignore the feedback completely.

Setbacks: When faced with setbacks, people with a fixed mindset will put the blame on others. They also get discouraged easily and are more likely to quit completely.

The Growth Mindset

Remember that these are all triggers that not only establish but also give away a fixed mindset.

Switching from one to the other can be hard but is possible. You need to watch out for these triggers because a fixed mindset can and will hold you back. Specific behaviors to move away from a fixed mindset can include the following suggestions:

• Listen to your inner voice- if you don't do so, it will rule your behavior in a habitual way, keeping you stuck where you are.

• When you find someone better than you, learn from them.

• When you are faced with a choice between something safe and something challenging, go for the challenge.

• When you hit a bump in the road, ask yourself what you can learn from it or what you can do next.

• When you receive feedback, don't get offended or take it as personal criticism. Think of ways how you can use this information to better your performance.

CHAPTER 5
THE POWER OF A GROWTH MINDSET

CHAPTER 5

The Power of a Growth Mindset

A growth mindset allows people to view themselves as capable of doing well in most, if not all settings. They definitely don't consider themselves as restricted by their current abilities, but believe that they can do whatever they want as long as they practice.

Consider the example of being given a new project, something that you haven't worked on before. Now your response could go either way.

You could look at this new challenge and think that you're not qualified to do this work or that such numbers, techs or designs weren't your cup of tea. This would obviously reflect a fixed mindset and you'd miss out on everything mentioned in the previous chapter.

However, you could also look at the same and start planning how you could make it work. You could deliberate what you'd need to bring to the table and what it would take to get the desired results.

This optimism and creativity indicate a growth mindset which will also empower you to gain the following:

Improvement Through Effort

A growth mindset allows people to believe that their basic abilities can develop through hard work and dedication. For this lot, brains and talents are merely the starting points and allow them to build on these.

This group of people exhibits an eagerness for learning and resilience which is a must for accomplishment. People with a growth mindset view their qualities as traits which can be developed through their commitment and effort.

Being of a growth mindset you're willing to try out new things because you know your success depends on your effort and not any innate ability. You're not focused on avoiding failure because you believe that if you do poorly you can improve and succeed in time.

The Growth Mindset

Plus research also indicates that growth mindset allows people to navigate stress and challenges better and lead to higher levels of wellbeing.

Offers A Sense Of Fulfilment

Unlike the fixed mindset, one of the most obvious benefits of the growth mindset are the endless opportunities to be availed. With a growth mindset, you continually pursue betterment followed by a sense of achievement and fulfilment.

A sense of achievement is also a precursor to a higher standard of excellence. In the process you learn that success is a continuous work in progress rather than instant gratification.

Develops Resilience

A growth mindset also lets you develop resilience. When you face challenges or setback, your mindset takes a more positive approach handling these.

The Growth Mindset

For instance, when you're given feedback, you know that it's an effective learning strategy that will help you set appropriate goals and standards for the future.

Buffers Against Demotivation

People with a growth mindset seek out opportunities and challenges to engage them rather than get their satisfaction from results. This means being motivated to do more and more.

Being more process oriented, rather than purely result oriented, these people thrive when they are in the process of doing something. The process presents a learning opportunity, stimulates them and drives them on to do even more.

As an example, rather than wishing for a completed book, written perfectly, the growth mindset is motivated to show up daily to work on it constantly until it is done, no matter what it takes. Instead of being fixated on a number on the scale, a growth mindset will focus more on working out every day to become more fit and healthy.

The Growth Mindset

Encourages Perseverance

A growth mindset also demands perseverance. The focus of a growth mindset is not to concentrate on what happens to you but on what happens for you.

Perseverance also means kicking fear of failure out the door. This amounts to taking chances when opportunity presents them and not limit yourself to living an overly cautious or paranoid life.

Tenacity is an essential ingredient for a growth mindset. And since you can't always have a 100% success rate with every challenge you tackle, tenacity will help reflect on your failures in the right manner.

Failure to find a solution usually opens up an opportunity for you to work on your skills and learn something new. When most people hit a wall, they either make an excuse or simply give up. However, a person with a growth mindset realizes that failure is an inevitable component of achieving success.

The Growth Mindset

As such they prepare for failure mentally, knowing that it will come at some time or the other. The thought neither scares them nor makes them give up.

Plus, allowing yourself to fail a little takes the pressure off of getting a perfect result every time.

Promotes Critical Thinking

When you talk about learning, making mistakes is a must because it forces you to identify where you made a mistake. This effort also helps you not only pinpoint a solution but also develop critical thinking.

Let's assume you get a somewhat tricky question in class. Should you switch off your brain because you feel overwhelmed, you'll never grow or learn anything.

However, if you acknowledge the problem by working it relentlessly, asking questions and evaluating critically, you have a better chance of finding an answer. At the same time, the effort that you put in will help your brain create new neural connections and become better equipped at solving similar problems. That's how you grow and be better at anything.

The Growth Mindset

Practice Makes Perfect

Not to overuse an age old cliché, but for a growth mindset practice does indeed make perfect, or more accurately a lot better at what you practice.

Since the growth mindset is triggered more by a dedication for learning as opposed to a yearning for approval, practice and effort promote qualities like creativity and intelligence. Individuals with

this mindset neither get discouraged by failure, nor do they consider themselves as failing but as learning.

In fact, practicing repeatedly does have a significant role in the learning process and is necessary to achieving expertise. One thing that most experts agree on is that training improves performance and changes the brain.

To summarize, a growth mindset sees the following situations as:

Skills: The growth mindset believes that skills are something that you can constantly change, improve and develop. Skills come from hard work so you can't stop working.

Challenges: The growth mindset is eager to embrace challenges and views them as an opportunity to grow. The chance to engage in a challenge makes the growth mind more persistent.

Effort: Effort is essential for a growth mindset and may even override talent. When the growth mindset sees effort as the path to success, it realizes the necessity for lifelong learning.

Feedback: The growth mindset views feedback as something constructive and an experience to learn from. It is an effective means to identify areas that need improvement.

Setbacks: Instead of putting a damper on things, setbacks are seen as ways to improve on current talents and efforts.

The Growth Mindset

CHAPTER 6
CAN YOU CHANGE YOUR MINDSET?

CHAPTER 6

Can You Change Your Mindset?

Beliefs can be changed when they no longer serve you or enable you to get to your goals.

Resistant To Change

Although mindsets can change, this only happens very slowly. This is especially true if you have long held beliefs about something. For instance, if you have been told that eating an apple a day is good for you, you may find it difficult to believe if someone told you otherwise.

Even though a fixed mindset is easy to form, it is resistant to change. Take the example of a stake holding a tent in its place in the ground. Although it can be moved, once it has been placed, you are reluctant to move it unless there is good reason to do so.

The Growth Mindset

So once you have formed a mindset about something, it conditions your future opinion about that thing. For instance, if you consider an upcoming event boring because the last one of the same kind was actually boring you may not want to go at all. However, if you do go and find it to be not boring at all, it may take you some time to change your mindset.

Using Fear To Change Your Mindset

An individual with a fixed mindset is more keen in looking smart than to fail when learning new things. They will do everything they can to avoid embarrassment and ignore what they truly lack of. In other words, they become fearful of looking stupid.

This in itself is an inhibiting factor. It's a possibility that this stems from a feeling of rejection or ridicule from childhood experiences or events stored in your unconscious mind that you may not even remember consciously.

As a result of this unconscious fear, your fixed mindset avoids trying new things, resists learning, stalls your development and may even make you act lazy.

The Growth Mindset

To counter this effectively and change your mindset, you need to become aware of the fear driving your behavior. And then realize that this fear has no basis in your present reality. You need to overcome it and let it go.

As an example, students with a fixed mindset view their intelligence level as unchanging. Their prime concern remains proving that they are smart, or hiding that they are not.

As such, they tend to avoid situations where they might fail. They also don't recover well from setbacks and only prefer engaging in tasks that they can already do well.

The same also reflects in others with this mindset where they limit themselves and sabotage their efforts.

Using Actions To Change Your Mindset

The Growth Mindset

Another approach to changing mindsets is through actions since skills and talents get developed through repetition and constant practice. The key to changing a fixed mindset is identifying and refuting the fixed mindset voice and taking growth oriented action repeatedly.

Although this isn't something that happens overnight, you can develop new skills through deliberate and repeated practice. And for every new skill that you develop, your fixed mindset voice weakens.

Identifying Your Counter Mindsets

Mindsets get formed through previous experiences and emotional milestones. But when these mindsets do not deliver the results you expect, they become counter mindsets.

This results in producing feelings of self-doubt, limiting beliefs and other negative thoughts that get in the way of progress. For the

most part, these negative thoughts occur so often that you may not even be aware of them.

The Growth Mindset

Think about that nudging voice which makes disparaging comments when you look in the mirror. It is the same voice which makes you unhappy with the way you look, makes you hesitate when approaching someone new or even when you want to consider a career change.

Now everyone experiences negative thoughts, or counter mindsets to a different degree, but the damage is collateral. It allows you to

habitually destroy your dreams and makes it very hard to remain positive. The only thing that remains are nasty reminders like "I can't talk to him/her", "I'm not smart enough for that", "I'm not qualified enough" or "I'm out of shape" and so on.

The Growth Mindset

To change your mindset, you need to pay attention to when this voice get raised and how often it happens. This will allow you to pinpoint the triggers of you counter mindset and narrow it down to a few key themes.

Shifting Gears From The Negative To The Positive

Once you have established your negative thoughts you need to prevent them from holding you back. Whenever a negative thought surfaces, counter it by giving an instant, yet positive reaction.

Say you want to go for a walk after dinner to get in more exercise. But the problem is that once dinner is over, you start hearing that voice that you're too tired, too full, or that it's too late to go out now.

Put a stop to that thinking pattern right away by getting up and putting on your walking shoes.

You will find that often just taking that first step is enough to turn off that nasty voice in your head.

The Growth Mindset

Understand "WHY" You Need To Change

Changing mindset requires a lot of willpower and hard work as formed habits aren't easy to break. This becomes even more challenging since many of the bad or limiting habits got formed when you were little and you have been doing things the same way ever since.

Understanding why you need to change a habit or mindset will make it more meaningful. Here two things should come in handy- motivation and willpower.

First, you'll need to rely on motivation to get you through changing your habits, and while the "why" will provide you with motivation, it can be hard to maintain in the long run. This is where willpower should step in and keep you going.

However, willpower can run out fairly quickly too. Think about trying to eat healthier and then you find a pack of Girl Scout cookies next to the fruit bowl at work. Maybe you get your willpower together and resist the cookies.

Next, you plan on going to the gym after work but need to stay behind for some reason. By the time you're done, you're not only tired but out of willpower as well. Plus, the fact that you weren't able to stick to your original plan doesn't help either.

So do you end up going to the gym or straight home? You probably know the answer because it happens to everyone.

So when you try to change your habits by relying on motivation and willpower alone, these might not be enough on their own. And that's also why so many people give up on changing their habits soon after they start, unable to follow through.

Instead what you need to do is to become a little forgiving and allow yourself some space to stumble. A fixed mindset leaves no allowance for mistakes leaving you emotionally drained and hesitant to try anything new.

The Growth Mindset

Start Small To Finish Big

One of the best ways to change mindsets is to start small towards big goals. Trying to become healthy, wealthy or wise along with more compassionate, calmer and successful is never easy. Once again you need to fight all your demons embedded in your mindset from those early years.

So if you find yourself stressed most of the time, try to meditate for two minutes every night before sitting in a lotus position for a straight half hour and a racing mind.

If you would like to become more fit, start with something as small as one push up only. Build your strength up along with your mindset before you get to an impressive set of twenty.

Decide on your tiny goal and pursue it with a positive mindset. Oftentimes, you may find that you actually do more then what you aimed for (maybe two to three push ups instead of one) and will feel great as you over achieve. On other days you may only achieve the minimum but still feel good since you met the goal.

Many people think that it's pointless to start so small but consistently hitting small goals successfully can help form new mindset habits.

CHAPTER 7: STRATEGIES TO DEVELOP A GROWTH MINDSET

CHAPTER 7

Strategies to Develop a Growth Mindset

When you let results such as your test scores, your weight, your job or your appearance define you, you become the victim of a fixed mindset. On the contrary, a growth mindset is all about learning and you can speed up the process by following some tried and true strategies.

Continual Learning

A growth mindset is foremost about evolving and growing. As such, instead of seeking approval from others, you need to surround yourself with people who can help you improve.

This means that you don't feel compelled to justify everything you do. Doing so only means you sacrifice your potential for growth. Instead prioritize your learning over approval as this will help you grow and succeed in your ventures.

The Growth Mindset

At the same time, trying new things will help you come up with different ideas and make you aware of what you are good at. You can also start challenging yourself with new tasks to develop your potential.

Be Committed

When you pair continual learning with commitment, you set yourself up for excellence.

Too often people make the mistake of wobbly commitment, thinking that they are committed to their cause or goal, but they're really not. With a shaky mindset, people set out to try things and then just wait to see what happens.

During the process many people only focus on the fact that they haven't yet accomplished their goal and can't stop thinking about how much further they have to go. This limiting mindset can sabotage your efforts making you more prone to giving up.

The Growth Mindset

However, when you develop a growth mindset, this problem gets eliminated. When you decide that you are fully committed to achieving your goals, regardless of any setbacks, you are more likely to succeed.

Here's a very simple, everyday example. You wake up late, jump out of bed, already stressed that you will miss your bus or your car pool. In the rush, you skip breakfast, dress hurriedly and rush out the door only to find that you have indeed missed your ride. Now a fixed mindset will likely respond by muttering, cursing, calling names and stay in a foul mood for the rest of the day.

But if you are working towards developing a growth, you will see this as an opportunity to commit to a more timely routine to make sure that this doesn't happen again.

You will then respond by going to bed early, setting an alarm and laying out your clothes in the evening so that tomorrow is better and different.

Don't just commit to planning it out in your head, but commit to carrying it out in action.

Develop Healthy Self Esteem

It can become very hard to aim for or achieve success without self- esteem. Before you can hope to grow or improve, you need to believe that you are capable of achieving your goal. Since you can't afford to undermine yourself, it becomes important that you stop worrying about what others think.

Your self-esteem is how you see yourself, a reflection of your mindset. It is created from an internal dialogue with yourself where you perceive and evaluate your worth whether positive or negative.

To have a strong self-esteem, you need a strong mindset, one that allows you to grow and evolve.

Work On Your Perspective

Every mindset has to do with perspective. Your foundational beliefs, thoughts, biases and attitudes all affect the way you process information and experience the world around you. Having a growth mindset increases the likelihood of formulating a winning perspective and achieving long term success.

Perspective is also the driving force behind motivation. Motivation determines whether you're able to achieve your set goals in long- term. It serves as a fuel to keep you going until you reach the finish line. Without motivation, you will lose the drive when faced with difficulties. The best way to keep your motivation burning is to remember your 'WHY' – Why did you start? Why is it important to you?

For instance, when you want to lose some weight, is it because you don't like how you feel in your current state or is it because you simply want to be healthy? While either reason will move you towards your goal, the one triggered by feeling of lack will possibly be more tenuous.

The Growth Mindset

Set Effective Goals

There are many factors that affect an individual's growth mindset.

One among these is setting effective and meaningful goals.

When goals are set realistically, it becomes more probable to achieve them. Achieving major goals or even smaller milestones towards a bigger goal is a positive learning process for the growth mindset.

A mind that is resilient will get you through the tough times and help you move on to the next challenge.

Manage Your Inner Negative Voice

One of the biggest obstacles to having a growth mindset is your inner critical voice. This voice keeps telling you that you can't do it, it's not worth it, you are who you are and you need to learn to live with that.

The Growth Mindset

This inner voice reinforces the idea that things are given and you've only got so much influence over your life. Everyone, even those with a growth mindset have this voice and to change your mindset you need to learn how to manage it.

As a starting point turn the "can't" in your mind into "can" and add a "yet" to the end of you sentences.

Facing Adversity

A growth mindset is successful in facing adversity. If you want to get through the rough patches, you will need to face each challenge head on.

If you avoid facing obstacles, you can't hope to maximize your current potential or develop new skills. Challenges present an opportunity to learn and expand which means that you can also grow in the process.

People with a growth mindset excel at challenges as these propel them forward.

Be Open To Feedback

A growth mindset always welcomes feedback as it is another chance to learn. Feedback also provides the opportunity to improve your performance. It helps you determine which areas you need to improve and where you're doing well.

And since feedback is provided by others, it's very important to interact with other people. Interacting or networking may involve stepping out of your comfort zone in order to inspire creativity.

Imagine reaching your office where your boss calls you in to complain about a report you've prepared or a project you're handling. With a fixed mindset, you will see this as a chance to beat yourself up. You may also end up feeling that you're not good enough for this job or that your boss is absolute clueless as to what it takes to get the job done.

In either case, the rest of your day is spent cribbing and complaining and in worst case scenarios, even job

The Growth Mindset

hunting. But when you strive to develop a growth mindset you'll see this same incident as something of a learning experience. You'll be more willing to evaluate your performance and seek constructive

feedback that actually helps you figure out how to improve your project. Instead of muttering and mumbling, moving on will be much easier.

CHAPTER 8
DEALING WITH SETBACKS

CHAPTER 8

Dealing with Setbacks

After debating the good and the bad about different mindsets, it becomes clearer that the way the mind responds to setbacks, disappointments or failure is very important.

For instance, for a fixed mindset a setback becomes a failure that distorts reality. This distorted view prevents people from seeing a situation for what it is. And without a clear picture of the situation, it can become impossible to pivot, solve or make any progress.

But for a growth mindset, this setback doesn't become overwhelming. In fact, it is often seen as something that will redirect your efforts in the right direction.

The Growth Mindset

The Importance Of Failure

For the go-getters, failure provides the opportunity to understand the gaps between what they wanted and the results they got.

For anyone interested in improving their performance and results in the future, a little setback can take them a long way forward. This is because the setback provides the chance to locate the cause of the mistake and then adapt future efforts accordingly.

Since it is important to realize that there will never be a situation where everything is perfect, it is equally important to expect setbacks on the way.

The growth mindset sees failure as a stepping stone from which it can learn the following valuable life lessons:

The Growth Mindset

Experience And Knowledge

The first important lesson learnt from a mistake, setback, or failure is experience. When you make a mistake, you take with you firsthand experience which helps you develop a deeper understanding.

The experience helps you alter your frame of mind and reflect on the real nature of things.

Another aspect of the same is that it brings with it firsthand knowledge. If you have growth mindset, you will use that knowledge in the future to overcome that very same failure.

Resilience And Growth

Setbacks also help build resilience. To become successful it is important that you know how to be resilient, so that your first instinct isn't to quit.

The same resilience also leads to growth where you learn to evolve in the face of adversity. Accepting that it's alright to experience an occasional setback allows you to recover from failure faster.

The Growth Mindset

Having said that remember while it's okay to fail, it's not okay to give up.

Change Your Strategy

Failure is an effective way to realize the need for change in your plans or strategies. While it is important to have a good plan in mind for success, it should not be set in stone.

Instead it should be flexible enough to allow you to review your approach, adjusting and measuring things as you move along. The important consideration in this aspect is that your goals should stay the same but your plan should constantly evolve.

Seeking Inspiration Through Others

As you have already seen, the growth mindset seeks inspiration through others who are better at something, more successful and get the desired results.

The Growth Mindset

You may start looking to well-known personalities from all walks of life and realize that every successful person has gone through a number of setbacks before achieving success.

Using Failure As Leverage

You can use any setback as leverage to not only recover from but also to propel forward. To leverage your setbacks, you need to know what you failed at and why. You also need to be aware of what you can do differently and how to avoid the same mistakes again.

This mindset will help you move past your mistakes instead of equating failure with complete defeat. With the right mindset you learn to grow and mature, gain new understanding and perspective on everything from love, life, business, money, relationships and people.

During this process, you're forced to make new connections and bridge gaps where you hadn't connected the dots before.

The Growth Mindset

Redefining Priorities And Values

Depending on your mindset, setbacks can either make you or break you. For the growth mindset, failure helps you reassess your priorities.

Once you realize that a setback is only a temporary hurdle, you learn to look beyond it. You start anew reordering things that are most important and shuffle others around. In an attempt to recover and improve yourself, you start to make the needed adjustments. At the same time, each subsequent failure also helps reshape values. Since the growth mindset centers on constant evolution and improvement, you will realize that what you valued ten years before is not what you value today.

It's a constant work in progress that learns to move ahead leaving setbacks behind.

Don't Let Your Failure Define You

When you come across a setback, it's tempting to let it shape the way you see yourself. For instance, a failed relationship may make you believe that you're not as attractive as you thought. Or a job you really wanted but didn't get, could make you believe that you're not that smart after all.

However, it's important to understand that your worth isn't determined by circumstance. A better option would be to assess your skills and strengths by thinking about major setbacks from the past.

Reviewing how you overcame those earlier obstacles can help devise a solid strategy.

Helps Reach Your Potential

For most people, failing means that they actually tried. They put forth effort to do something worthwhile which didn't work out. But both trying and failing can become valuable teachers for anyone with a growth mindset. Failure promotes better thinking and prepares you to maximize your potential for future efforts.

The same also builds you up in ways you never thought possible by allowing you to take responsibility for your mistakes. Often times, it's hard to realize what you're capable of until you push through failures. This also helps in developing your potential.

The Growth Mindset

Failure Is Always Better Than Regret

Failing is a much better alternative to regretting. Think about living with regret not knowing what could've happened had you applied for that job. And then compare it with failing to secure the job but finding out where your shortcomings lay. At least with the failure option you're closer to getting it right the next time.

Success that comes easy often leave tons of room for failure as it makes you feel that nothing could go wrong. But failure helps you not underestimate success and try harder next time. Regret, on the other hand, provides no such opportunity and only leaves you feeling dismal.

Setbacks Yield A Sense Of Direction

Most people keep second guessing the decisions they take. They do so not because these decisions are right or wrong but only because they aren't sure how things light pan out.

The Growth Mindset

But should a decision hit a setback, it points to a path for redirection. Now a growth mindset is quick to grab this opportunity and learns from its mistakes. It develops a sense of clarity on where things went wrong and how to redirect your efforts to correct the mistake.

And because redirection takes you into new venues, you get to explore more options and step out of your comfort zone. In this sense, failure can also help you get rid of the fear of stepping out of your comfort zone.

CONCLUSION

Now you know that a growth mindset allows you to take on bold challenges without the element of fear. And even you are likely to encounter tough times, armed with the right mindset, you become more resilient. You also become more accepting when things go wrong but your focus shifts to identifying a solution rather than running away from uncertainty.

In essence, when you develop a growth mindset, you become a happier and healthier person who is not afraid to seek out new opportunities to continue on the path to self-improvement. Just remember that goals are a good thing to have but can become destructive if you place too much value on them and too little on the road to achieving them.

You have the power to choose which way you want to follow. If you're not satisfied with how you feel about yourself or your life, you can change your mindset to one that will let you grow and thrive.

THANK YOU FOR READING MY BOOK!

DID YOU LIKE THIS BOOK?

Before you leave, I wanted to say thank you again for buying my book. I know you could have picked from a number of different books on this topic, but you chose this one so I can't thank you enough for doing that and reading until the end. I'd like to ask you a small favor. If you enjoyed this book or feel that it has helped you in anyway, then could you please take a minute and post an honest review about it on Amazon?

Click here to post a review!

Your review will help get my book out there to more people and they'll be grateful, as will I

ABOUT THE AUTHOR

I'm Ana Smitt and I believe that every person can achieve the body of his or her dreams, and I work hard to give everyone that chance by providing workable, proven advice grounded in science, not a desire to sell phony magazines, workout products, or supplements.

Through my work, I've helped thousands of people achieve their Healthy Lifestyle and Fitness Goals, and Self Improvement. I share everything I know in my books.

So if you're looking to get in shape and look great, then I think I can help you. I hope you enjoy my books and I'd love to hear from your review

Sincerely,

Ana Smitt

My Author Page

MORE BOOKS YOU MIGHT LIKE

	**High Intensity Interval Training (HIIT)** Discover HIIT How To Quickly Melt Your Extra Fat, Build Muscle, And Get In The Best Shape Of Your Life With High Intensity Interval That Take Just Minutes…
	**High Intensity Interval Training Workouts:** Fit In 15, Discover The Step-By-Step System For Women To Lose Weight Safely & Effectively with High Intensity Interval Training Workouts
	**Brain Health Brain Training** Brain Health Brain Training: How To Nurture And Nourish Your Brain For Top Performance In Every Aspect Of Your Life with Brain training and Brain Health

The Growth Mindset

www.ingramcontent.com/pod-product-compliance
Lightning Source LLC
Chambersburg PA
CBHW020602220526
45463CB00006B/2419